Wet and Dry

By Jack Challoner

Contents

Wet and Dry 3
What Is Wet? 4
What Is Dry? 6
Clouds and Rain 8
Rain and Rivers 10
The Ocean 12
Keeping Water Out 14
Plants and Water 16
Animals and Water 18
Wet Air 20
Getting Dry 22
Water in Food 24
In the Rain Forest 26
Desert Plants 28
Desert Animals 30
Glossary and Index 32

RSVP®

RAINTREE
STECK-VAUGHN
PUBLISHERS
The Steck-Vaughn Company

Austin, Texas

Published by Raintree Steck-Vaughn Publishers, an imprint of Steck-Vaughn Company

Editors: Kim Merlino, Kathy DeVico
Project Manager: Lyda Guz
Electronic Production: Scott Melcer

Photo Credits: cover: NHPA: top Lutra;
Planet Earth Pictures: bottom John Lythgoe;
Bubbles: p. 20 Ian West;
Bruce Coleman: p. 21 (bottom) Chris James;
FLPA: p. 11 (center) Martin Withers; p. 13 (top) D. P. Wilson;
pp. 17 (center), 31 E. & D. Hosking; p. 18 P. Berry; p. 19 A. Wharton;
NHPA: p. 27 Stephen Dalton;
Oxford Scientific Films: p. 8 John Downer;
p. 29 Tony Martin; p. 30 Eyal Bartov;
Planet Earth Pictures: pp. 10, 12, John Lythgoe;
p. 13 (center) G. Van Ryckevorsel;
Science Photo Library: p. 9 (top) Keith Kent;
p. 11 (top) Martin Bond; p. 26 Dr. Morley Read;
p. 28 Sinclair Stammers;
Stock Boston: p. 3 Peter Vandermark.

All other photographs by Claire Paxton.

Library of Congress Cataloging-in-Publication Data

Challoner, Jack.
Wet and dry / by Jack Challoner.
p. cm. — (Start-up science)
Includes index.
ISBN 0-8172-4322-4
1. Water — Experiments — Juvenile literature. [1. Water — Experiments.   2. Experiments.]   I. Title   II. Series: Challoner, Jack.
Start-up science.
QC920.C48 1997
500 — dc20
95-30014
CIP
AC

Printed in Spain
Bound in the United States
1 2 3 4 5 6 7 8 9 0 LB 99 98 97 96

Wet and Dry

This book will answer lots of questions that you may have about wet things and dry things. But it will also make you think for yourself.

Each time you turn a page, you will find an activity that you can do yourself at home or at school. You may need help from an adult.

We all know that water is wet. When we play with water, we get wet, too. But what is water, and where does it go when we dry ourselves? How do we stay dry when it rains?

What Is Wet?

Water makes things wet. We use water every day to wash. Our eyes need to stay wet all the time. What things do you know that are wet?

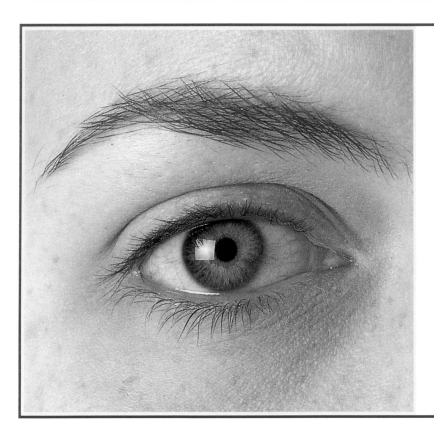

Wet eyes

Our eyes need to stay wet. A special watery mixture washes over the fronts of our eyes each time we blink. We blink about 20 times every minute.

Did you know?

The smallest amount of water is called a water **molecule**. Molecules are very small. There are more of them in one drop of water than there are people in the whole world.

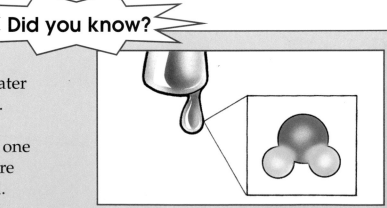

Frozen water

Snow and **ice** are dry. When snow and ice melt, they become liquid water again. The water from them is wet.

Water for washing

How do you use water in the bathroom? This boy is washing his face with water. Where else can you see water in this picture?

Now try this

Sponges can hold large amounts of water. They are useful for washing.

You will need:
a sponge, a sink full of water, a measuring cup

1. Soak the sponge in the water.

2. Lift it out of the water, and wait until it stops dripping.

3. Squeeze the sponge over the measuring cup. How much water comes out?

What Is Dry?

What things are dry?
The clothes you are wearing?
Your hair? When wet things
become dry, where does the
water go?

Fallen leaves

Many trees drop their leaves
for the winter. Once a leaf
has fallen from a tree, it no
longer gets any water.
These leaves have dried
up on the forest floor.

Hot air

Some people use blow-dryers to dry their hair. The warm, dry air from a blow-dryer takes the water away faster than a towel.

Dry clothes

Clothes are hung up to dry after they have been washed. When dry, they are folded and ready to wear.

Now try this

When it is warm, water quickly disappears. It **evaporates** to become part of the air.

You will need:

two saucers, some water, a teaspoon

1. Put about one teaspoon of water in each of the saucers.

2. Put one saucer somewhere warm and the other saucer in the refrigerator.

3. Look at the saucers every few hours. Which water evaporates first?

Clouds and Rain

Have you ever wondered what **clouds** are made of? Each cloud is made of tiny water droplets. When the droplets join, the water falls from the sky as drops of rain.

A wet day

In some parts of the world, called the **tropics**, it rains nearly every day. The rain is warm and falls very heavily.

Did you know?

The wettest places in the world have more than 430 inches (11 m) of rain each year. The extra water runs into rivers and oceans.

430 inches (11 m)

Dark clouds

This thunderhead is made up of tiny droplets of water and bits of ice. There is enough water in this cloud for a huge rainstorm.

Down the drain

Water that falls on roads and paths stays there as puddles or washes down drains, like this one.

Now try this

A cloud is made up of tiny water droplets. These droplets join together to make drops that fall as rain.

You will need:

a plant sprayer, a large ground-floor window

1. Stand outside the window, and make sure it is closed.

2. Make sure that the sprayer makes a fine mist. Spray water all over the window.

3. Keep spraying until drops form and run down the window.

Rain and Rivers

Have you ever seen a river? Much of the water that falls as rain finds its way to rivers. What happens to a river if there is not enough rain, or if there is too much rain?

Did you know?

Water joins a river all along the way, but each river has a place where it starts. This place is called its **source**. The sources of most rivers are in mountains.

Dried-up river

Many people use the water in rivers for washing, cooking, and for fun. But when there is not enough rain to keep a river full of water, the river can dry up.

Flooded river

When too much rain falls, it can make a river overflow its banks. People living near a river have to move away because water from the river floods their homes.

Riverbanks

The sides of a river are called its banks. Riverbanks are home for many plants and animals that depend on the river water.

Now try this

Water always flows downhill, but rarely in a straight line.

You will need:
some sand, a brick or stone, water in a jug, a wooden board

1. Do this outside. Cover the board with sand.

2. Lift one end of the board onto the brick so that it slopes.

3. Trickle water slowly onto the top of the board in one place. Watch how the path of the water bends.

The Ocean

If you have been to the seashore, you know that ocean water is salty. Water flows into the ocean from rivers. There are many different types of plants and animals in the ocean. They all need to stay wet.

Did you know?

Most of the Earth is covered with water. There is ice at the North and South poles. Most of the rest of the water is in the oceans.

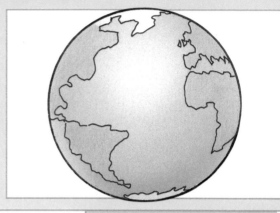

Into the ocean

Rivers are made of water. They grow bigger and bigger and sometimes join together. Finally, most of the river water flows into the ocean.

Clinging shells

These are limpets. When the tide goes out, they are left on dry rocks. They cling to the rocks, and stay wet inside their shells until the tide returns.

Fish in the ocean

All fish need to stay in water because they cannot breathe in the air. Salmon like these sometimes live in the ocean and sometimes in rivers.

Now try this

Salt **dissolves** in water.

You will need:
water, a clear drinking cup, salt, a spoon

1. Fill half the cup with cool tap water.

2. Put a spoonful of salt in the water, and stir until it seems to disappear.

3. Count the number of spoonfuls of salt you can add before no more will dissolve.

4. Rinse the cup, and fill it halfway

with warm tap water. See how many spoonfuls of salt will dissolve in it now.

Keeping Water Out

Which clothes do you wear in the rain? Some of our clothes are **waterproof**. This means that they do not let water through. Do you have waterproof clothes?

Rainy days

On rainy days, we sometimes wear clothes that are made from waterproof plastic. This girl is wearing a plastic coat and hat, and rubber boots on her feet.

Did you know?

The wet suits that divers wear do not keep water out — they keep water in. The trapped water is warmed by the diver's body, and helps the diver to stay warm in the water.

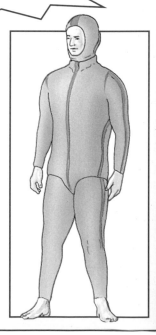

Ducks in water

Ducks spend most of their time in the water. Their feathers need to be waterproof, so that most of their body stays warm and dry.

Duck feathers

Ducks have feathers that are covered in an oily liquid. The oil makes the feathers waterproof because oil and water do not mix.

Now try this

You will need:
a jug of water, food coloring, vegetable oil, a drinking glass

1. Fill the drinking glass halfway with vegetable oil.

2. Add a few drops of food coloring to the jug of water.

3. Carefully put drops of the water into the oil. The drops will not mix with the oil.

Plants and Water

All plants need water. Without it, they die. Some plants live in water. Other plants grow in soil and take in water through their roots.

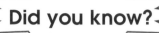
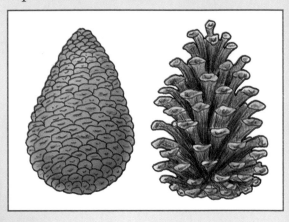

Underground

Most plants send long roots down into the soil, in search of water. Water from the soil goes up the roots and into the plant. The water carries food that the plant needs with it.

Pond plants

These plants find the water they need easily because they live in a pond.

Strong roots

Most plants die if they have too much water. These trees are called **mangroves**. Their strong roots keep them out of the water, so they do not get too wet.

Now try this

Without water, seeds cannot grow into plants.

You will need:
two saucers, seeds (mung beans, watercress, or grass seeds), tissues

1. Place a tissue on each saucer. Drip a little water on one tissue, to make it damp. Do not put too much water on it.

2. Now put about ten seeds on each tissue. Leave the saucers in a light place.

3. Drip water onto the wet saucer every day, but leave the other one dry. What happens?

Animals and Water

Like plants, all animals need water to live. Some animals, such as whales and fish, live in water. Others live on land and find the water they need in lakes, ponds, and rivers.

Finding water

Like you, other animals need water for drinking and washing. Many animals drink from ponds or lakes. These are often called **watering holes**.

Did you know?

Earthworms spend most of their time underground. But when it rains, they come to the surface so that they do not drown.

Wet skin

Animals such as frogs spend some of their life in the water and some of it on land. We call an animal like this an **amphibian**.

Now try this

Birds and other animals need food and water to live.

You will need:
a shallow tray or dish, water, birdseed

1. Put the tray on the ground in your yard or school yard.

2. Fill the tray with water. Put some birdseed next to it.

3. Go indoors, and watch the tray. After a few days, birds may come to eat the seeds and drink the water.

Wet Air

Usually water in the air is in the form of a gas called **water vapor**. Water vapor particles are too small to see. As the air cools, the particles join to form droplets of liquid water that you can see.

Steam breath

Did you know?

A small town in Chile collects water from the air! Large plastic sheets collect water from **fog** that forms over the mountain daily.

There is water vapor in your breath. On a winter day, when it is cold, the vapor becomes drops of water. These drops look like steam from a kettle.

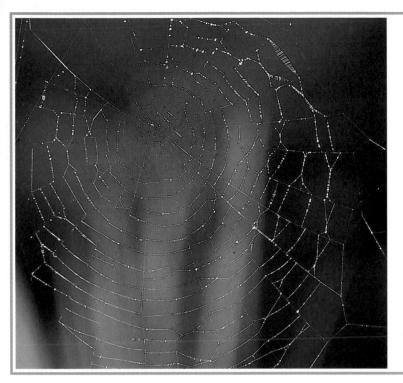

Dewdrops

Have you ever seen **dew**? You can see it on grass, and on spiders' webs on some cold mornings. Dew is tiny drops of water from the air.

Clouds of water

Next time you are in a mist or fog, you will know what it is like to be in a cloud. Just like clouds, fog is made of tiny drops of water in the air.

Now try this

When wet air touches a cold surface, water drops appear.

You will need:
a drinking glass, some ice cubes

1. Make sure the glass is dry on the inside and on the outside.

2. Put the ice cubes in the glass.

3. Wait for a minute. Now feel the outside of the glass.

Getting Dry

After a bath or a shower, how do you dry yourself? You probably use a towel. But how does a towel work? What other ways are there to get dry?

Did you know?

After taking a bath or a swim, you often feel cold, even on a hot day. This is because the water takes heat away from your skin when it evaporates.

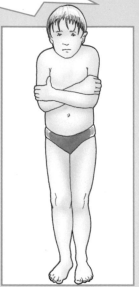

Warm and dry

Clothes dry quickly on a warm, windy day. The water evaporates into the air.

Shaking dry

When dogs are wet, they shake themselves to get rid of the water. Most people use towels to dry themselves. Towels are made of tiny fibers that soak up the water. A towel can hold lots of water.

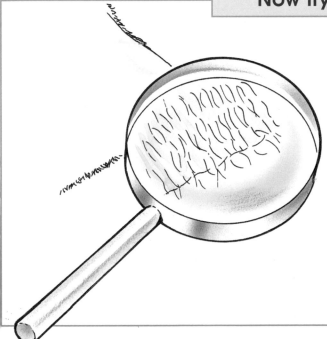

Now try this

The fibers of a tissue **absorb** water. This means that they soak up the water.

You will need:
a tissue, a hand lens, a saucer, some water

1. Tear the tissue in half. With the hand lens, look at a torn edge. What can you see?

2. Pour water into the saucer. Touch the water with the edge of the tissue. What happens?

23

Water in Food

What have you eaten today? Do you think the food had water in it? Most foods contain water, but some are dry.

Wet foods

Our bodies need water. Some of this water comes from the food we eat. Some foods, such as fruit, have a lot of water and feel wet. Others, such as chocolate, feel dry.

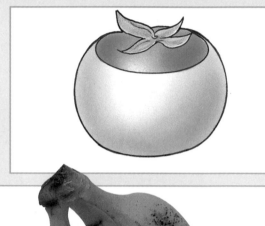

Dried foods

Some of the foods we eat are dried so that they can be stored. Milk can be dried to a powder. When the right amount of water is added, the powder becomes liquid milk again.

Now try this

Do foods with more or less water spoil faster?

You will need:
two pieces of bread, a plastic bag

1. Put one piece of bread in the plastic bag, and close it tightly. Leave the other one out in a dry place.

2. After a day or so, the bread you left out should be dry — all its water will have evaporated.

3. Look at the two pieces of bread each day for the next two weeks.

BE SAFE!
Do not open the plastic bag to touch, taste, or smell the bread.

In the Rain Forest

Some of the warmest and wettest places in the world are **rain forests**. Many different types of plants and animals live there.

Warm and wet

Rain forests have so much rain that the ground is soft and damp, and the air is always full of water.

Did you know?

Because rain forests are so wet, lots of trees grow close together. Animals communicate by making loud noises, because they cannot see each other in the dark.

Tree frog

A frog's skin needs to stay wet. The skin of this tree frog gets water from the damp air. It lays its eggs in pools of water in the leaves of rain forest trees.

Now try this

You can make your own rain forest leaves and fill them with water.

You will need:
aluminum foil, a plant sprayer

1. Make lots of different leaf shapes from the foil.

2. Now spray water on the foil. Do this over a sink or bowl.

3. Water will collect in some parts of the foil. Which shapes are best for collecting water?

Desert Plants

The deserts of the world are very dry places. In the summer, they are very hot during the day. Desert plants have special ways of getting water and keeping it.

Desert water

An **oasis** is a part of the desert where water from under the ground comes to the surface. Many plants and animals live in an oasis like the one above.

Waxy surface

A cactus is thick and has a waxy surface. This helps it hold in water. Desert animals often try to eat cactuses for their water. But the cactus has spikes on its surface that may stop them.

Now try this

Many desert plants have leaves that keep in water.

You will need:
a paper bag, a small plastic bag, two tissues

1. Fold both tissues in half, and drip water onto each one to make them damp.

2. Wrap one tissue in the paper bag. Wrap the other tissue in the plastic bag.

3. Leave the bags somewhere warm. After a few hours, which tissue is still wet?

Desert Animals

All animals need water. In the desert, there is very little water. The animals of the desert store water in their bodies. They eat plants or other animals to get water.

Storing water

People can die if they don't drink for a few days. But this camel can go for weeks without drinking water, because it hardly ever sweats.

Did you know?

A camel can drink more than 27 gallons (100 l) of water. That is enough water to fill a bathtub!

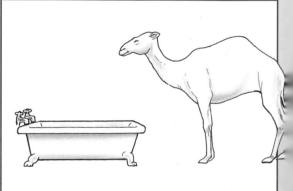

Seed eater

Like many other small desert animals, gerbils get most of their water from the seeds of desert plants.

Now try this

You can find water in seeds by crushing them.

You will need:
tissues, mustard seeds, a wooden spoon

1. Put some mustard seeds on the tissue.

2. Press the seeds firmly with the wooden spoon to crush them.

3. Lift the tissue up so the seeds fall off. You should find a little water left behind on the tissue.

Glossary

absorb to soak up a liquid

amphibian an animal that lives its adult life on land but whose young live in water

cloud many tiny droplets of water in the air

dew tiny drops of water from the air that form on cool surfaces

dissolve to mix evenly throughout a liquid

evaporate to change from a liquid to a gas

fog a cloud near to the ground

ice frozen water

mangrove tropical trees that grow in swamps with their roots above the water

molecule a very small particle, the smallest bit of something

oasis a place in the desert where there is water

rain forest a tropical forest where there is a lot of rainfall

source a place where a stream or river starts

tropics parts of the world where it is hot and wet

watering hole a pool of water where animals drink and bathe

waterproof able to keep water from getting through

water vapor invisible water in the air

Index

absorb 23
amphibians 19, 27
animals 11, 12, 13, 18–19, 23, 26, 27, 28, 29, 30–31

birds 15, 19
blow-dryers 7

clothes 6, 7, 14, 22
clouds 8–9, 21

deserts 28–31
dew 21
dissolving 13

Earth 12
evaporation 7, 22
eyes 4

feathers 15

fish 13, 18
floods 11
fog 20, 21
food 24–25
freezing 5

ice 5, 9, 12

mangroves 17
melting 5
mist 21
molecules 4, 20
moon 6

oasis 28, 29
ocean 8, 12

plants 6, 11, 12, 16–17, 18, 24, 26, 28, 29, 30

rain 8–9, 10, 14, 26
rain forests 26–27
rivers 8, 10–11, 12, 13
roots 16, 17

seeds 16, 17, 31
snow 5
sponges 5

towels 7, 22, 23
tropics 8

washing 4, 5, 10, 18
watering holes 18
waterproof 14, 15
water vapor 20

Copy- 1-99-
$14.98